Run, Swim and Fly

By Menglin Zhao
Illustrated by Michael Magpantay

Library For All Ltd.

Library For All is an Australian not for profit organisation with a mission to make knowledge accessible to all via an innovative digital library solution. Visit us at libraryforall.org

Run, Swim and Fly

This edition published 2022

Published by Library For All Ltd
Email: info@libraryforall.org
URL: libraryforall.org

Library For All gratefully acknowledges the contributions of all who made previous editions of this book possible.

This book was made possible by the generous support of Save The Children.

Save the Children

Original illustrations by Michael Magpantay

Run, Swim and Fly
Zhao, Menglin
ISBN: 978-1-922827-79-1
SKU02674

Run, Swim and Fly

A horse can run.

A rabbit can run.

A bear can run.

Fish cannot run,
but it can swim.

A butterfly cannot run,
but it can fly.

Birds cannot run,
but they can fly.

You can use these questions to talk about this book with your family, friends and teachers.

What did you learn from this book?

Describe this book in one word. Funny? Scary? Colourful? Interesting?

How did this book make you feel when you finished reading it?

What was your favourite part of this book?

download our reader app
getlibraryforall.org

About the contributors

Library For All works with authors and illustrators from around the world to develop diverse, relevant, high quality stories for young readers. Visit libraryforall.org for the latest news on writers' workshop events, submission guidelines and other creative opportunities.

Did you enjoy this book?

We have hundreds more expertly curated original stories to choose from.

We work in partnership with authors, educators, cultural advisors, governments and NGOs to bring the joy of reading to children everywhere.

Did you know?

We create global impact in these fields by embracing the United Nations Sustainable Development Goals.

3 GOOD HEALTH AND WELL-BEING	4 QUALITY EDUCATION	5 GENDER EQUALITY
8 DECENT WORK AND ECONOMIC GROWTH	9 INDUSTRY INNOVATION AND INFRASTRUCTURE	10 REDUCED INEQUALITIES	11 SUSTAINABLE CITIES AND COMMUNITIES
12 RESPONSIBLE CONSUMPTION AND PRODUCTION	13 CLIMATE ACTION	16 PEACE, JUSTICE AND STRONG INSTITUTIONS	17 PARTNERSHIPS FOR THE GOALS

libraryforall.org

www.ingramcontent.com/pod-product-compliance
Lightning Source LLC
Chambersburg PA
CBHW040321050426
42452CB00018B/2961